MUSICIANSHIP
FOR THE
OLDER BEGINNER

by James Bastien

The Bastien Older Beginner Piano Library

PREFACE

MUSICIANSHIP FOR THE OLDER BEGINNER is designed to be used as a companion book to **THE OLDER BEGIN-NER PIANO COURSE.** Theory, Technic, and Sight Reading materials are correlated unit by unit to the basic course. It may also be used with any other piano course.

The **Theory** portion contains a combination of written exercises and keyboard harmony.

The **Technic** portion is designed to develop hand and finger coordination and facility, and to develop ease and control at the keyboard. Dynamics and tempo are to be suggested by the teacher. Transposition is indicated for some exercises; additional transposition may be suggested at the teachers' discretion.

The **Sight Reading** portion provides additional reading to reinforce new concepts. A variety of reading experiences is provided to relieve monotony. The student should give a brief pre-study analysis before playing: 1) tap or clap the rhythm; 2) observe the clef, key and time signature. While playing he should 1) keep his eyes on the music; 2) look ahead; 3)keep going. Transposition may be assigned at the teacher's discretion.

This balanced program will provide the student with a thorough beginning music program in basic fundamentals.

Suggested Use of Materials with **THE OLDER BEGINNER PIANO COURSE, LEVEL 2**

When the student reaches **page 5,** he is ready to begin . . . . **Musicianship, Level 2** (WP35)
When the student reaches **page 21,** he is ready to begin . . . . **Favorite Melodies the World Over, Level 2** (WP38)
When the student reaches **page 33,** he is ready to begin . . . . **Easy Piano Classics** (WP42)
When the student reaches **page 37,** he is ready to begin . . . . **Pop, Rock 'N Blues, Book 2** (GP38)
When the student reaches **page 45,** he is ready to begin . . . . **Scott Joplin Favorites** (GP90)

©1977 Kjos West, San Diego, California
Any reproduction, adaptation or arrangement of this work in whole or in part
without the consent of the copyright owner constitutes an infringement of copyright.
All Rights Reserved. International Copyright Secured. Printed in U.S.A.

Published by Kjos West.
Distributed by Neil A. Kjos Music Company.
National Order Desk, 4382 Jutland Dr., San Diego, CA 92117

ISBN 0-8497-5032-6
Cover Photo: Harry Crosby/Photophile

CONTENTS

UNIT 1
THEORY

WRITING MAJOR SHARP KEY SIGNATURES

To write the Major sharp key signatures:

Write the sharps in their order until you write the sharp BEFORE the keynote.

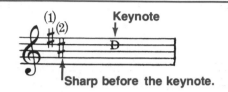

1. Write these Major key signatures.

A G D E A D

BASS STYLES

Various kinds of bass accompaniment styles can be used to harmonize melodies. Here is one BROKEN CHORD BASS pattern in which the notes of the chords are played one-at-a-time.

2. Write this bass pattern for measures 2 through 7. If no chord symbol is given for a measure, use the same chord from the previous measure. Play this piece. Transpose it to the suggested keys.

Transpose: G, F, D, A, E

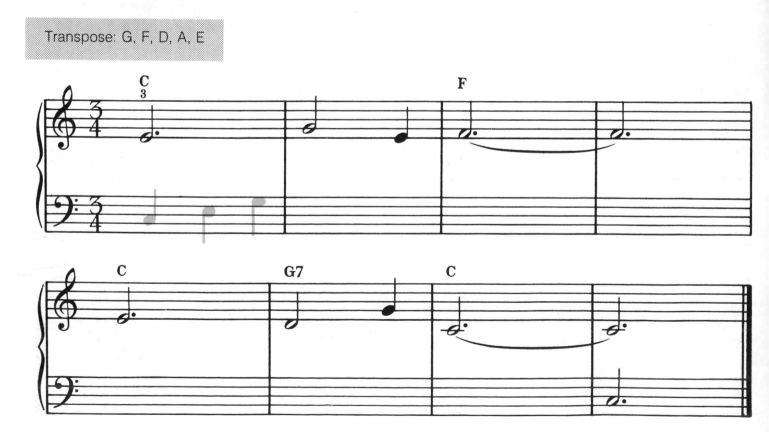

Here is another BROKEN CHORD BASS pattern.

3. Write this bass pattern for the blank measures. Play this piece. Transpose it to the suggested keys.

Transpose: G, C, D, A, E

HOME, SWEET HOME

Through man - sions and pal - a - ces though — we may roam, Be it

ev - er so hum - ble, there's no ——— place like home.

Here is a WALTZ BASS pattern.

4. Write this pattern for the blank measures. If no chord symbol is given for a measure, use the same chord from the previous measure. Play this piece. Transpose it to the suggested keys.

Transpose: F, G

BEAUTIFUL DREAMER

STEPHEN FOSTER

Beau - ti - ful dream - er, wake un - to me, ———

Star - light and dew drops are wait - ing for thee. ———

TECHNIC

BASS STYLE EXERCISES

First, practice the bass part alone as a warm-up exercise; transpose it to the suggested keys. Next, play the exercise; transpose it to the suggested keys.

1. Transpose: F, G, D, A, E

2. Transpose: C, G, D, A, E

3. Transpose: F, C, D, A, E

LEGATO · STACCATO STUDY

4. Transpose: C, D, G, A, E

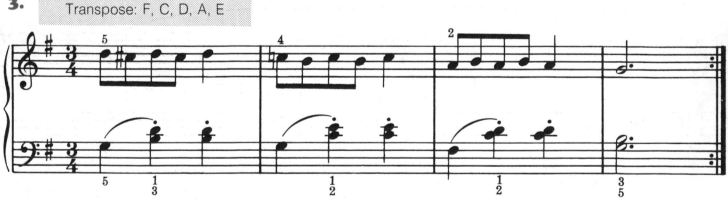

SIGHT READING

1.

SILENT NIGHT
(Grüber)

Slowly

2.

AULD LANG SYNE
(Scotch Song)

Moderato

3.

LA MATTINATA
(Leoncavallo)

Moderato

UNIT 2
THEORY

SYNCOPATION

SYNCOPATION means to stress or accent weak beats. Often a LONG note is placed on a weak beat. This syncopated rhythm pattern is "short - long — short."

1. Tap and count this rhythm.

2. Make up (improvise) a melody in the rhythm given. Use notes in the D Major scale. Write your melody on this staff.

INTERVALS

3. Draw notes above the given notes to form the correct intervals. Play these intervals.

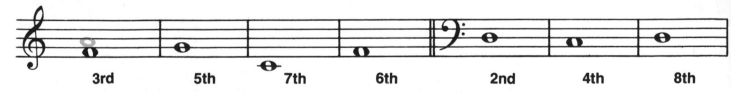

MAJOR · MINOR CHORDS

4. Name and play these Major and minor chords.

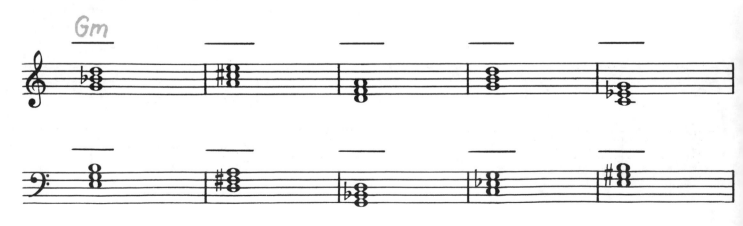

QUESTION AND ANSWER PHRASES

Make up (improvise) two-measure answer phrases to complete these lines. Write your best "answers" on the staffs.

HARMONIZING LEAD LINES

The chord symbols used in the next piece are the Primary Chords of the scale:

| G = I chord | C = IV chord | D7 = V7 chord |

Play **COMIN' THRO' THE RYE**, harmonizing (chording) with your Left Hand. Always play a Left Hand chord on the first beat of each measure. If no chord symbol is given in the next measure, repeat the same chord from the measure before.

COMIN' THRO' THE RYE

Robert Burns
(Scottish Folk Song)

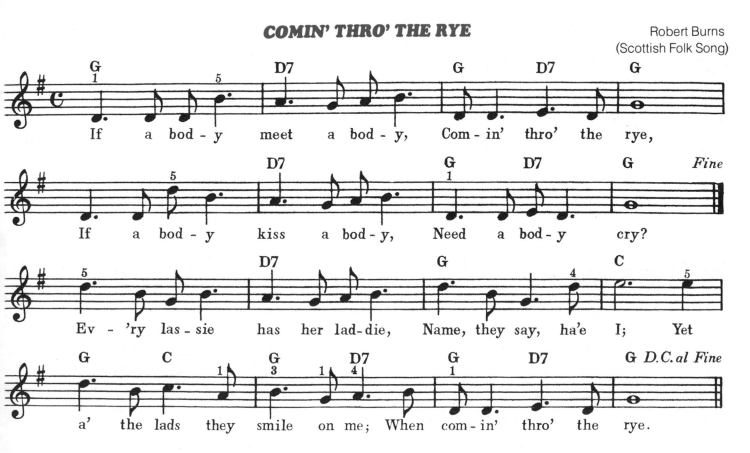

TECHNIC

MAJOR · MINOR CHORD STUDIES

SIGHT READING

1.

2.

3.

OH, THEM GOLDEN SLIPPERS
(Bland)

UNIT 3
THEORY

RELATIVE MINOR SCALES

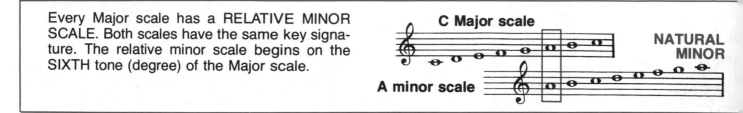

Every Major scale has a RELATIVE MINOR SCALE. Both scales have the same key signature. The relative minor scale begins on the SIXTH tone (degree) of the Major scale.

1. Write the D natural minor scale. It is the relative minor scale of F Major. (Both scales have the same key signature.) Play this scale.

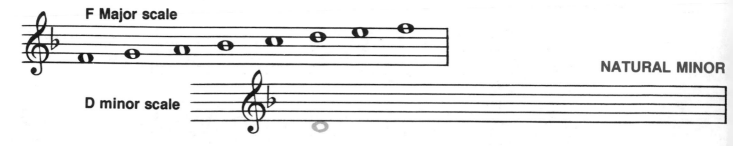

FORMS OF MINOR SCALES

Each Major scale has only ONE form.
Each minor scale has THREE forms: **(1) NATURAL**   **(2) HARMONIC**   **(3) MELODIC**

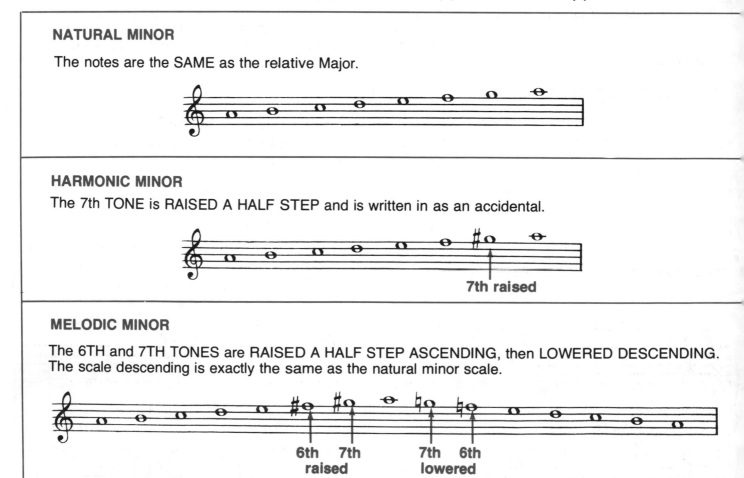

NATURAL MINOR

The notes are the SAME as the relative Major.

HARMONIC MINOR

The 7th TONE is RAISED A HALF STEP and is written in as an accidental.

MELODIC MINOR

The 6TH and 7TH TONES are RAISED A HALF STEP ASCENDING, then LOWERED DESCENDING. The scale descending is exactly the same as the natural minor scale.

Write the harmonic and melodic forms of the E minor scale. Play all three scales.

NATURAL

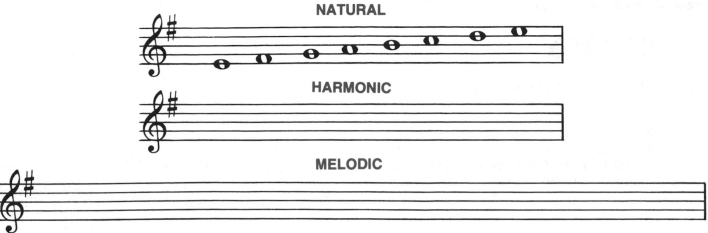

HARMONIC

MELODIC

Change these natural minor scales to HARMONIC MINOR scales by writing an accidental in the correct place. Play these scales.

B minor scale

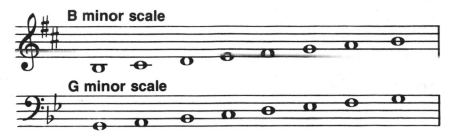

G minor scale

MINOR KEY SIGNATURES

Both the relative Major and its relative minor key have the SAME signature. To tell whether a piece is in Major or minor, look at the first and last notes. These are CLUES which help tell Major or minor. Also, listen to see if the piece sounds Major or minor. If the piece sounds minor, you can find the minor key name with this rule:

Count DOWN THREE HALF STEPS from the Major key name.

Write the minor key name on the blanks.

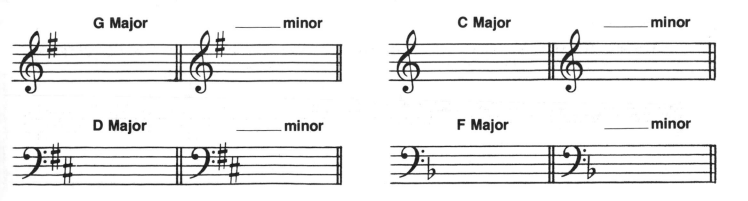

TECHNIC

A MINOR SCALE AND CHORD STUDIES

Contrary Motion
Transpose: d, e minor

1.

Primary Minor Chords
Transpose: d, e, c minor

2.

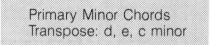

A MINOR ETUDE

3.

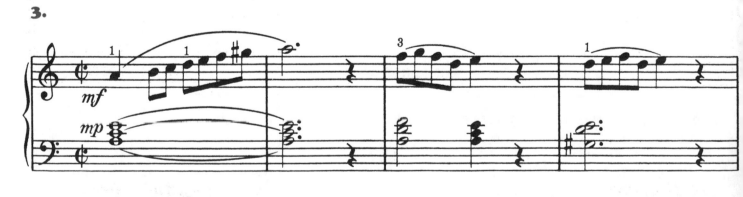

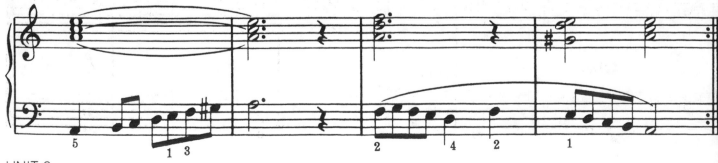

SIGHT READING

1.

2.

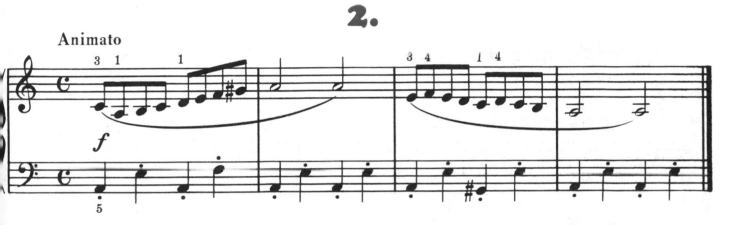

3.

4.

UNIT 4
THEORY

TRIPLET RHYTHM

A triplet figure is usually indicated by a *3* and a slur.
A triplet eighth note figure is equal to one quarter note.

The triplet rhythm may be counted in various ways:

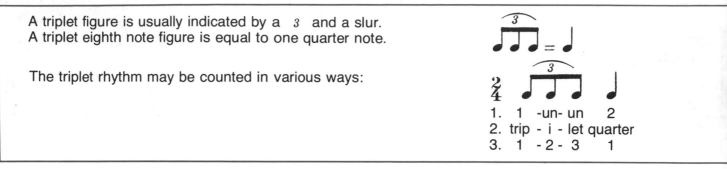

1. 1 -un- un   2
2. trip - i - let quarter
3. 1 - 2 - 3   1

1. Tap and count this rhythm.

2. Make up (improvise) a melody in the rhythm given. Use notes in the G Major scale. Write your melody on this staff.

QUESTION AND ANSWER PHRASES

3. Make up (improvise) answer phrases to these question phrases. Write your best "answers" on the staffs.

4. Write a melody and the harmony indicated by the chord symbols to complete these lines.

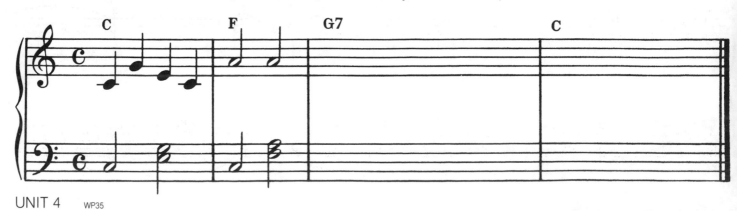

MAJOR - MINOR KEY SIGNATURES

5. Look at the first and last notes in each melody. Play each melody and listen to the sound. Write the Major or minor key name on the blanks.

Key of _____

Key of _____

Key of _____

Key of _____

HARMONIZING LEAD LINES

6. Play **THE ASH GROVE,** harmonizing (chording) with your Left Hand. Always play a Left Hand chord on the first beat of each measure. If no chord symbol is given in the next measure, repeat the same chord from the measure before.

THE ASH GROVE

WELSH FOLK SONG

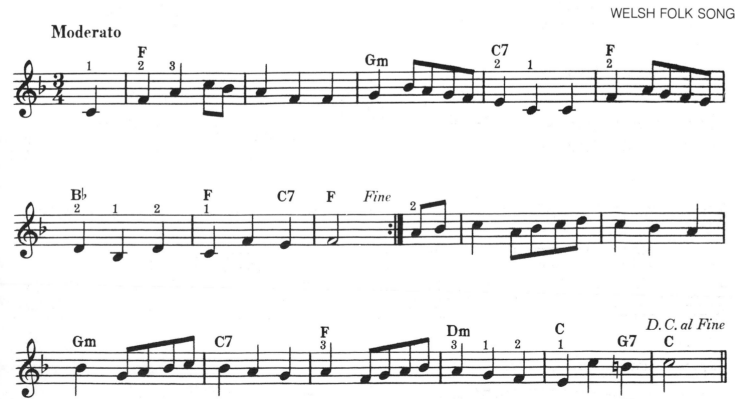

TECHNIC

TRIPLET RHYTHM STUDIES

1. Transpose these studies to other keys.

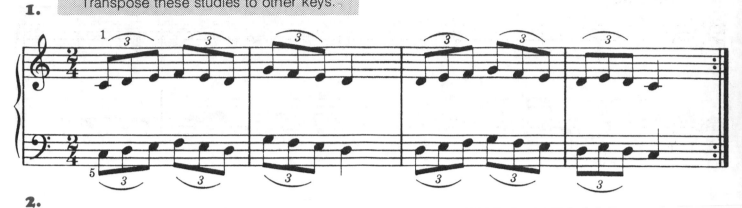

2.

3. D MINOR ETUDE

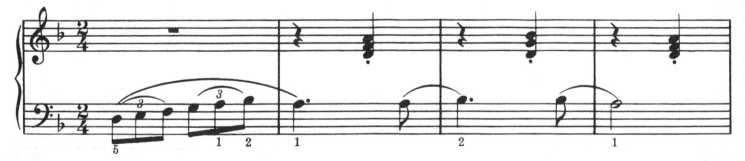

SIGHT READING

1.

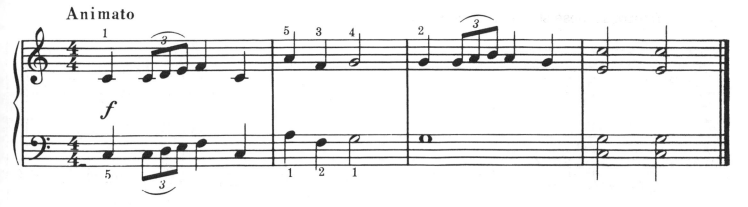

2.

THEME FROM THE FIFTH SYMPHONY
(Tchaikovsky)

3.

4.

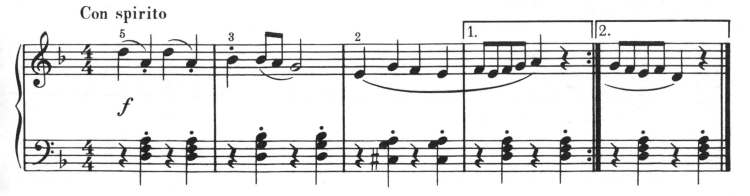

UNIT 5
THEORY

SCALE - TONE INTERVALS

The intervals of the C Major scale are shown below. Notice that the 2nd, 3rd, 6th, and 7th intervals are called MAJOR intervals. The Prime, 4th, 5th, and 8th intervals are called PERFECT intervals. These intervals are the same for all Major scales.

Perfect Prime	Major 2nd	Major 3rd	Perfect 4th	Perfect 5th	Major 6th	Major 7th	Perfect 8th (octave)

1. Name these harmonic intervals of the scale. Write **M** for Major, **P** for Perfect. Play these intervals.

P5 _____   _____   _____   _____   _____   _____

2. Name these intervals. Think of the scale to which each interval belongs. Play these intervals.

_____   _____   _____   _____   _____

ALTERED INTERVALS

An interval of the scale which is RAISED or LOWERED is called ALTERED. All intervals can be altered.

Major intervals which are RAISED are called AUGMENTED (larger).

Augmented 6th

M6   A6

Major intervals which are LOWERED are called MINOR (smaller).

minor 3rd   minor 6th

M3   m3   M6   m6

3. Name the following intervals. Write **M** for Major, **m** for minor, **A** for Augmented. Play these intervals.

_____   _____   _____   _____   _____   _____

TRIADS AND INVERSIONS

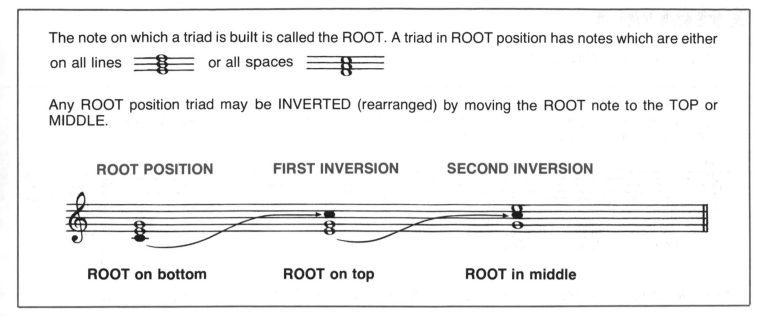

The note on which a triad is built is called the ROOT. A triad in ROOT position has notes which are either on all lines or all spaces.

Any ROOT position triad may be INVERTED (rearranged) by moving the ROOT note to the TOP or MIDDLE.

4. Write the inversions of these triads. Play all three chords in each key.

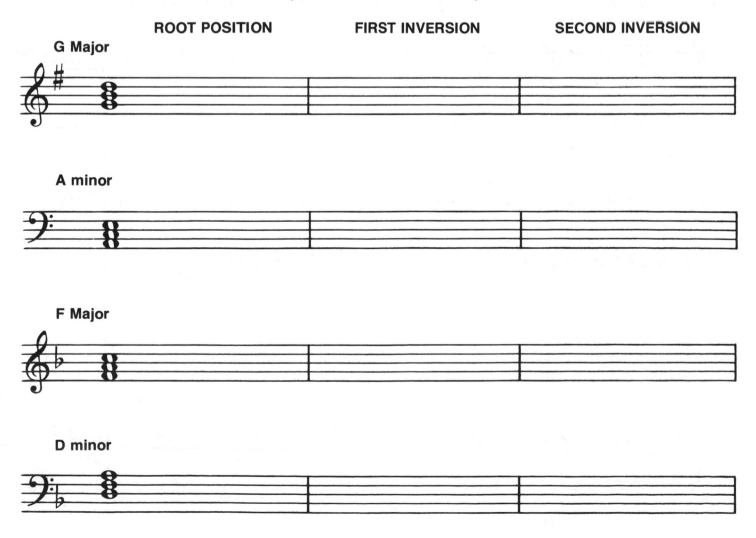

TECHNIC

TRIAD AND INVERSION STUDIES

Transpose to other Major and minor keys.

1.

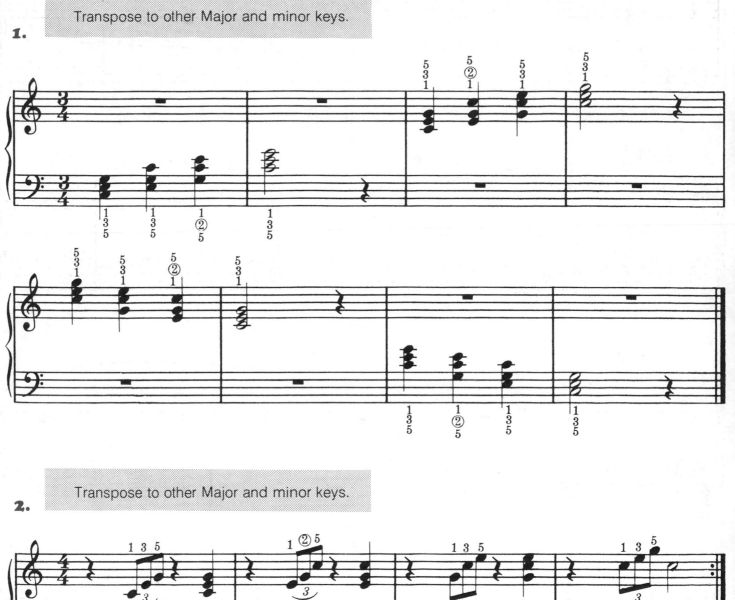

Transpose to other Major and minor keys.

2.

Transpose to other Major and minor keys.

3.

SIGHT READING

1.

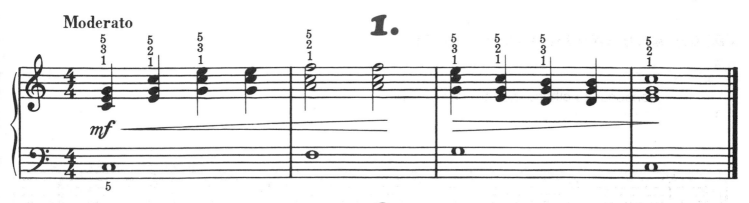

2.

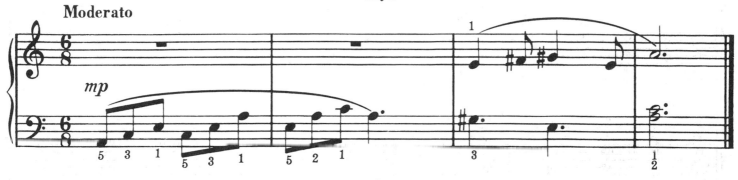

3.

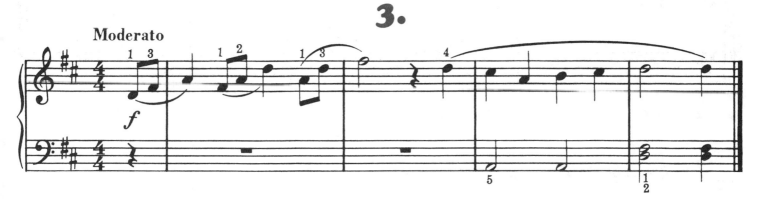

4.

5.

UNIT 6
THEORY

THE ORDER OF FLATS

The flats are ALWAYS written in the same order on the staff.

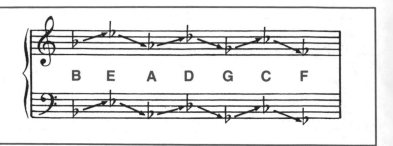

B E A D G C F

1. Write the order of flats three times on this staff.

MAJOR FLAT KEY SIGNATURES*

To find the Major key name of a piece with flats in the key signature:

1. Look at the NEXT-TO-LAST flat.

2. The letter name of this flat is the name of the Major key.

B♭ Major

EXCEPTIONS

F Major (one flat)   C Major (no sharps or flats)

2. Name these Major key signatures.

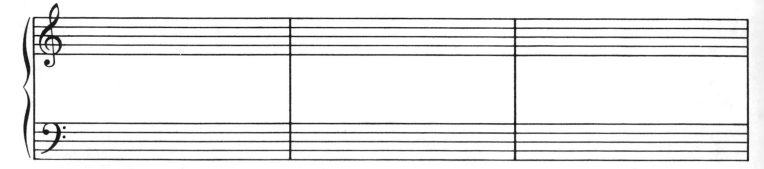

WRITING MAJOR FLAT KEY SIGNATURES

To write the Major flat key signatures:

Write the flats in their order until you write one MORE flat than the keynote (Exception: F Major).

3. Write these Major key signatures.

Bb   Ab   Eb   Db   F   Ab

GROUP 3 KEYS (Db, Ab, Eb)

The GROUP 3 KEYS are Db, Ab, and Eb. Each of the I chords is formed with a pattern of "black — white — black" keys.

black		black
	white	

4. Write the I chords in the Group 3 Keys. Add the necessary flats. Play these chords.

Db Major   Ab Major   Eb Major

The five finger positions for Db and Ab have only one white key. Eb is the unusual key in Group 3, because there are two white keys in the five finger position.

5. Write the notes in each five finger position for the Group 3 Keys. Add the necessary flats. Play these positions.

Db Major   Ab Major   Eb Major

TECHNIC

GROUP 3 FIVE FINGER STUDIES*

Practice hands separately at first. Play the Left Hand one octave lower than written.

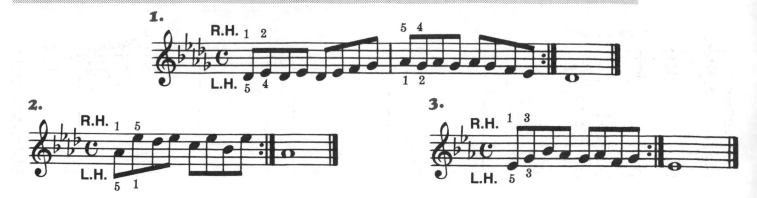

GROUP 3 CHORD STUDIES

Practice hands separately at first. Play the Right Hand one octave higher than written.

*The scales of D♭, A♭, and E♭ are written on page 45.

SIGHT READING

1.

Con anima

2.

TURKEY IN THE STRAW
(Barn Dance)

Spiritoso

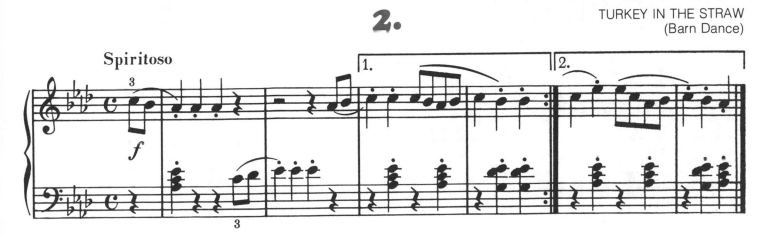

3.

BLOW THE MAN DOWN
(Sea Chanty)

Lively

UNIT 7
THEORY

RECOGNIZING INVERTED TRIADS

> FIRST INVERSION TRIADS have two notes at the bottom close together (to form an interval of a THIRD).
>
> The ROOT is always the TOP note of the interval of the FOURTH.

1. Find the FIRST INVERSION triads in this group. Circle the ROOT and write the root name of each first inversion triad. Play these chords.

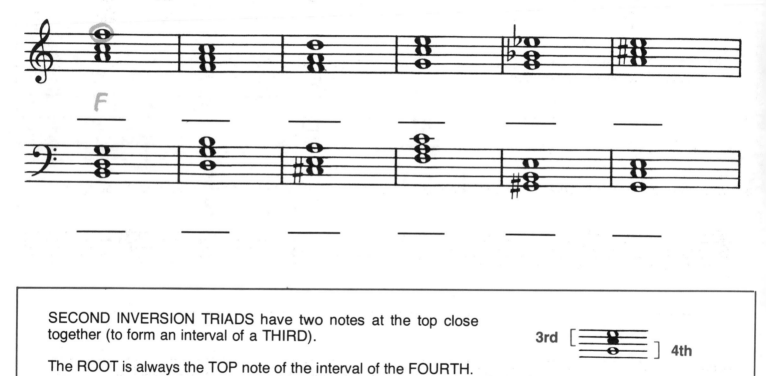

> SECOND INVERSION TRIADS have two notes at the top close together (to form an interval of a THIRD).
>
> The ROOT is always the TOP note of the interval of the FOURTH.

2. Find the SECOND INVERSION triads in this group. Circle the ROOT and write the root name of each second inversion triad. Play these chords.

ALTERED INTERVALS

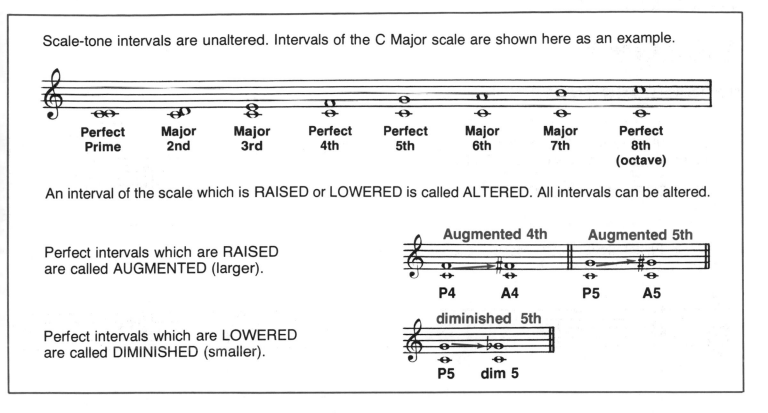

Scale-tone intervals are unaltered. Intervals of the C Major scale are shown here as an example.

| Perfect Prime | Major 2nd | Major 3rd | Perfect 4th | Perfect 5th | Major 6th | Major 7th | Perfect 8th (octave) |

An interval of the scale which is RAISED or LOWERED is called ALTERED. All intervals can be altered.

Perfect intervals which are RAISED are called AUGMENTED (larger).

Perfect intervals which are LOWERED are called DIMINISHED (smaller).

3. Name the following intervals. Write **P** for Perfect, **A** for Augmented, **dim** for diminished. Play these intervals.

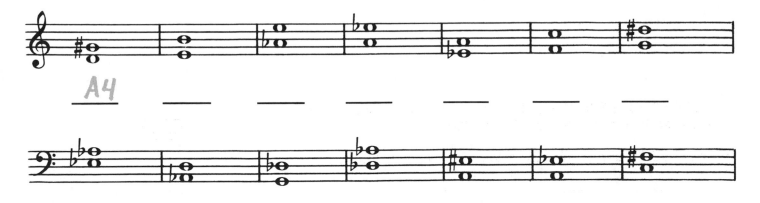

4. Draw notes above the given notes to form the correct intervals. (M = Major, m = minor; see page 20.) Play these intervals.

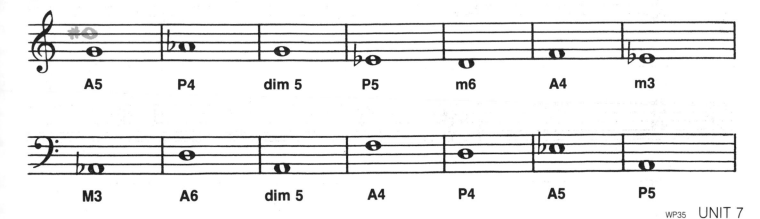

A5   P4   dim 5   P5   m6   A4   m3

M3   A6   dim 5   A4   P4   A5   P5

TECHNIC

FIRST INVERSION TRIAD STUDIES

Practice hands separately at first. Play the Left Hand an octave lower than written.

1.

2.

3.

SECOND INVERSION TRIAD STUDIES

4.

5.

6.

SIGHT READING

1.

Lively

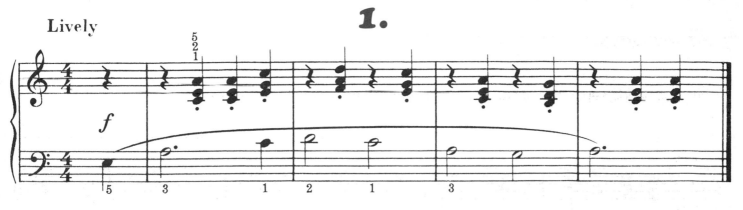

2.

GO DOWN, MOSES
(Spiritual)

Slowly

3.

Andante con moto

WP35 UNIT 7

UNIT 8
THEORY

SIXTEENTH NOTES

Four sixteenth notes equal one quarter note:

The four sixteenth notes are often divided:

A single sixteenth note has TWO FLAGS.

Two or more sixteenth notes are connected by a DOUBLE BEAM.

Sixteenth notes may be counted in various ways:

1. 1- ee- and - a   2
2. 4 six- teenth notes quarter
3. 1   2   3   4   1

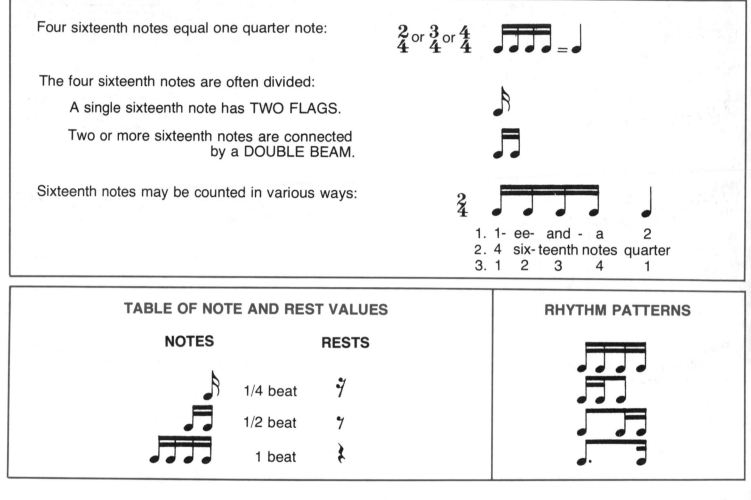

TABLE OF NOTE AND REST VALUES

NOTES	RESTS
1/4 beat	♪
1/2 beat	♪
1 beat	♪

RHYTHM PATTERNS

1. Tap and count this rhythm.

2. Make up (improvise) a melody in the rhythm given. Use notes of the D Major scale. Write your melody on this staff.

3. Play and count this melody.   **Key of____**

This rhythm pattern ♩♫ has a "long, short, short" feel.

This pattern may be counted: ♩♫

        1 and da

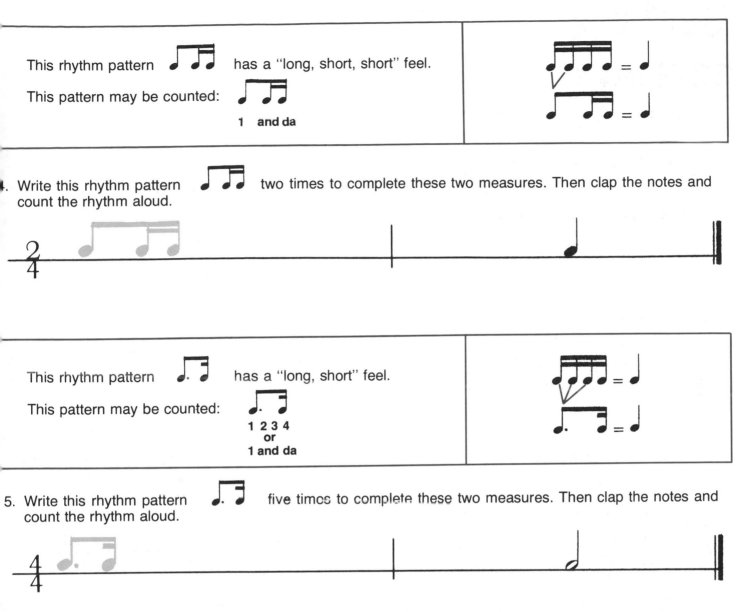

4. Write this rhythm pattern ♫ two times to complete these two measures. Then clap the notes and count the rhythm aloud.

This rhythm pattern ♩.♪ has a "long, short" feel.

This pattern may be counted: ♩.♪

        1 2 3 4
        or
        1 and da

5. Write this rhythm pattern ♩.♪ five times to complete these two measures. Then clap the notes and count the rhythm aloud.

6. Clap the rhythm to **CAMPTOWN RACES.** Play the melody and count aloud. Play again and harmonize the melody; count aloud as you play.

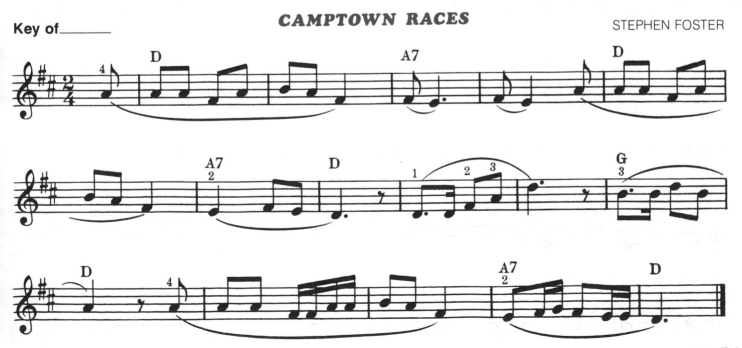

CAMPTOWN RACES

STEPHEN FOSTER

Key of_____

TECHNIC

SIXTEENTH NOTE STUDIES

Transpose the first four studies on this page to other keys.

1.

2. Trill

3.

4.

Double Notes

5.

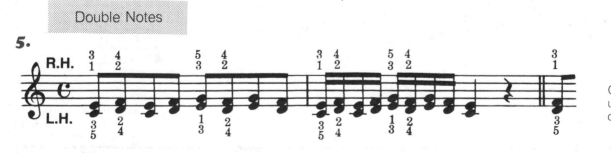

Continue this pattern
up the keyboard
on the white keys.

6.

Continue this pattern
up the keyboard
on the white keys.

SIGHT READING

1.

Con anima

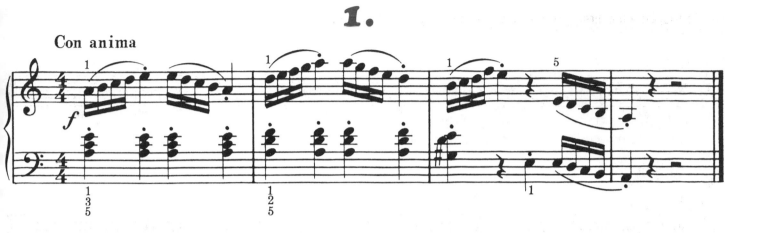

2.

Gracefully

3.

Tempo de marcia

4.

March tempo

TOREADOR SONG FROM "CARMEN"
(Bizet)

UNIT 9
THEORY

AUGMENTED TRIADS

The word AUGMENT means to make LARGER.

An AUGMENTED TRIAD is formed by RAISING the top note (5th) of a Major triad one half step.

Measured from its root, an Augmented triad has intervals of a Major 3rd and an AUGMENTED 5th:

Also, an Augmented triad has TWO Major 3rd intervals:

1. Write an Augmented triad for each Major triad given. Play these chords.

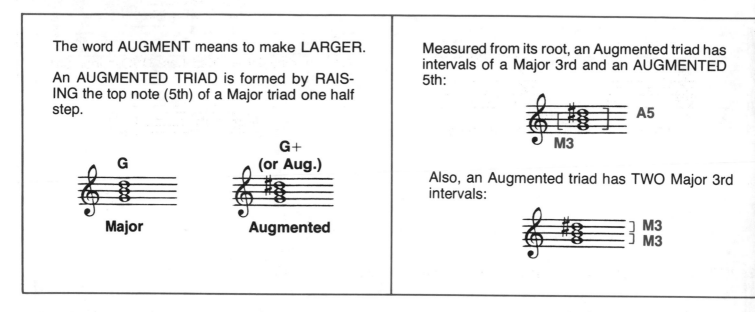

2. Name the following triads. Use a capital letter for Major; use a capital letter with + for Augmented. Play these chords.

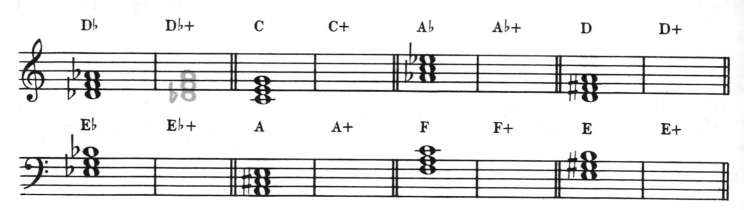

DIMINISHED TRIADS

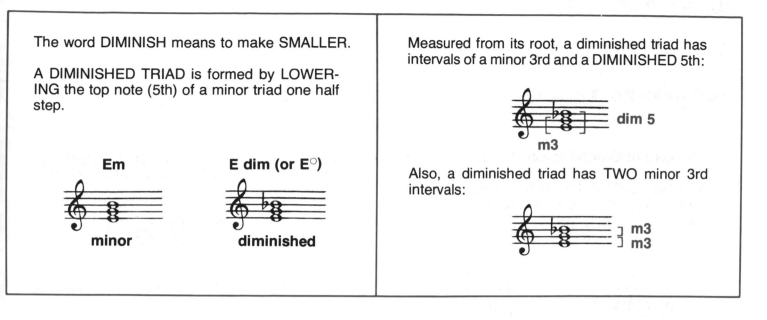

The word DIMINISH means to make SMALLER.

A DIMINISHED TRIAD is formed by LOWERING the top note (5th) of a minor triad one half step.

Em — minor

E dim (or E°) — diminished

Measured from its root, a diminished triad has intervals of a minor 3rd and a DIMINISHED 5th:

dim 5
m3

Also, a diminished triad has TWO minor 3rd intervals:

m3
m3

3. Write a diminished triad for each minor triad given. Play these chords.

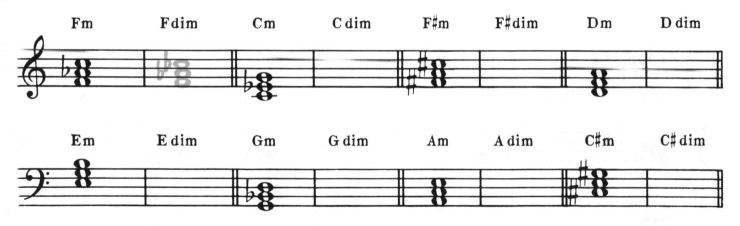

| Fm | F dim | Cm | C dim | F#m | F#dim | Dm | D dim |

| Em | E dim | Gm | G dim | Am | A dim | C#m | C# dim |

4. Name the following triads. Use a capital letter with **m** for minor; use a capital letter with **dim** for diminished. Play these chords.

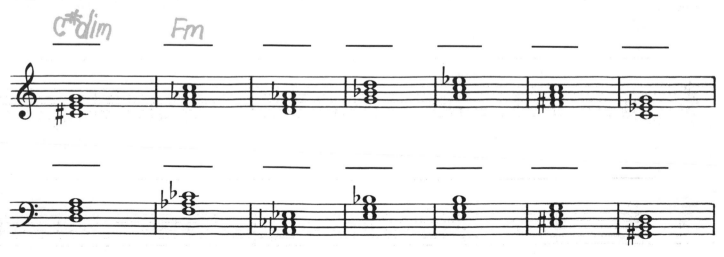

C#dim   Fm

TECHNIC

AUGMENTED TRIAD STUDIES

1.

2.

Transpose: A♭, E♭, and other keys

3.

DIMINISHED TRIAD STUDIES

4.

5.

Transpose to other minor keys.

6.

SIGHT READING

1.

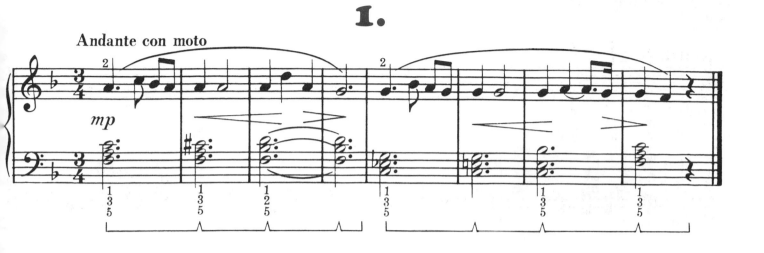

2.

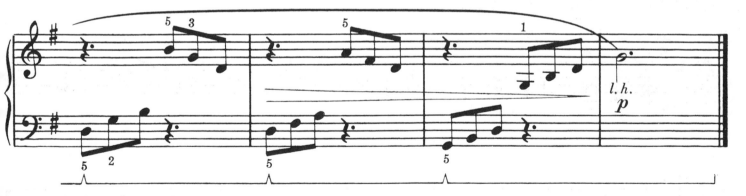

3.

UNIT 10
THEORY

GROUP 4 KEYS (G♭,B♭,B)

1. The GROUP 4 KEYS are G♭, B♭, B. Each I chord in this group has a DIFFERENT look and feel. Play these chords.

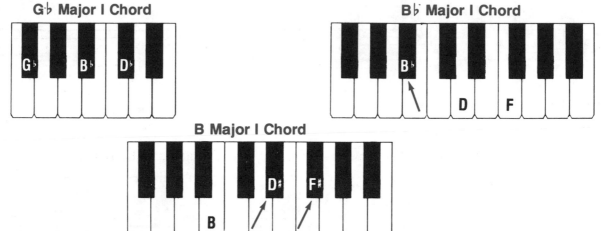

2. Draw these I chords on the staff. Add the necessary sharps or flats. Play these chords.

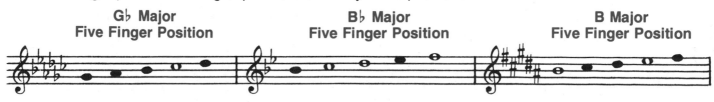

3. Each five finger position in this group is different. Play these positions.*

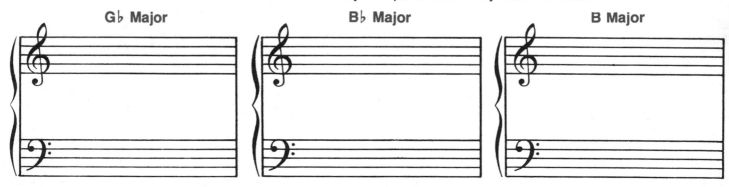

4. Draw the notes of these five finger positions on the staff. Add the necessary sharps or flats. Play these positions.

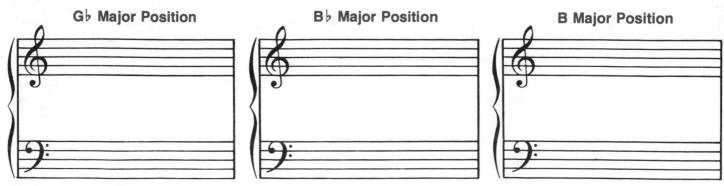

*The scales of G♭, B♭, and B are written on page 45.

UNIT 10   WP35

NAMING AND WRITING CHORDS

5. Name these root position triads. Play these chords.

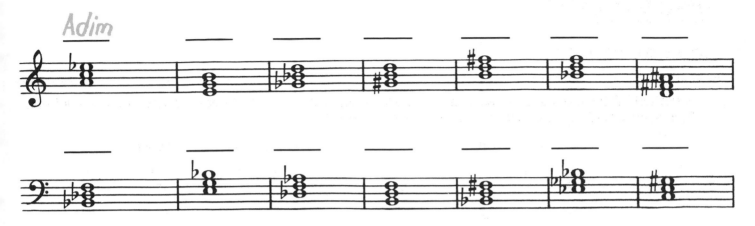

6. Draw these root position triads. Play these chords.

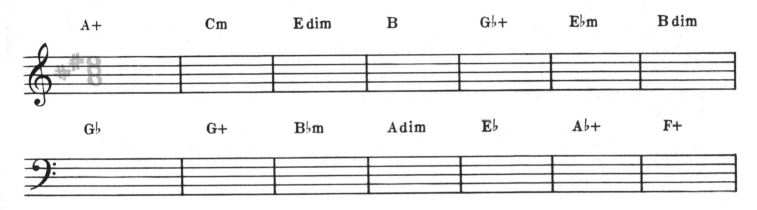

| A+ | Cm | E dim | B | G♭+ | E♭m | B dim |

| G♭ | G+ | B♭m | A dim | E♭ | A♭+ | F+ |

7. Name these inverted triads. Play these chords.

8. Draw these inverted triads. Play these chords.

| D | Cm | E | G♭ | B♭m | Fm | E♭ |

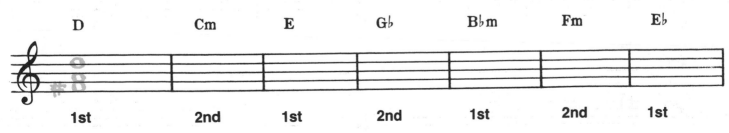

| 1st | 2nd | 1st | 2nd | 1st | 2nd | 1st |

TECHNIC

GROUP 4 CHORD STUDIES

Practice hands separately at first.

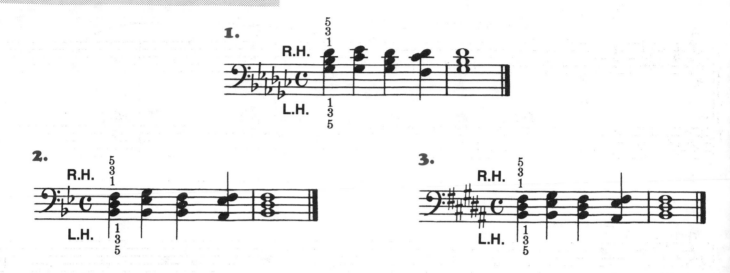

CHORD PROGRESSIONS

Practice the following chord progressions in all keys chromatically up the scale. Play hands separately at first. Think ahead for each new position. Practice each chord progression until you know it well.

Tonic, Subdominant, Tonic, Dominant Seventh, Tonic

Major, Augmented, Major, minor, Major

minor, diminished, minor, Dominant Seventh, minor

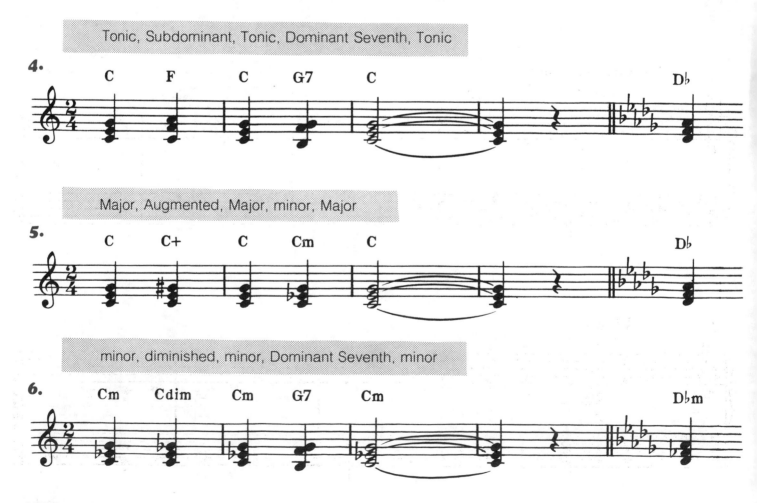

SIGHT READING

1.

MOLLY MALONE
(English Folk Song)

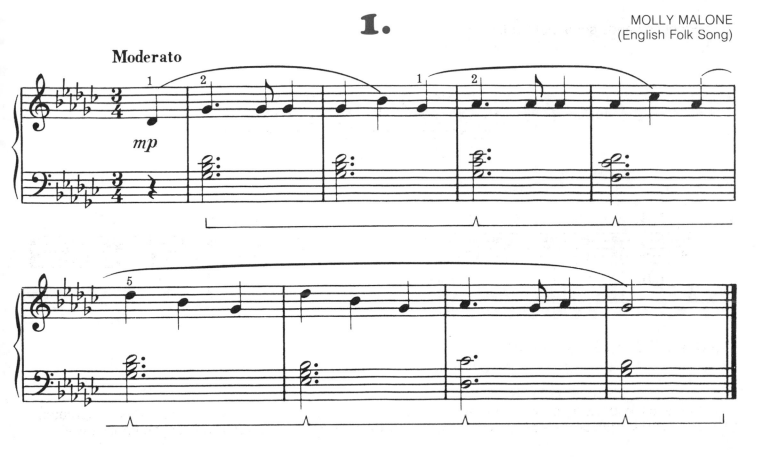

2.

ROCK OF AGES
(Toplady)

3.

REFERENCE
CADENCES

A CADENCE is a chord progression which marks a close or conclusion at the ends of phrases, sections, or at the end of the entire piece. Cadence is a Latin word which means "to fall." Cadences mark the "falls" (points of rest) in music.

Practice these cadences, first hands separately, then together. Play in all keys.

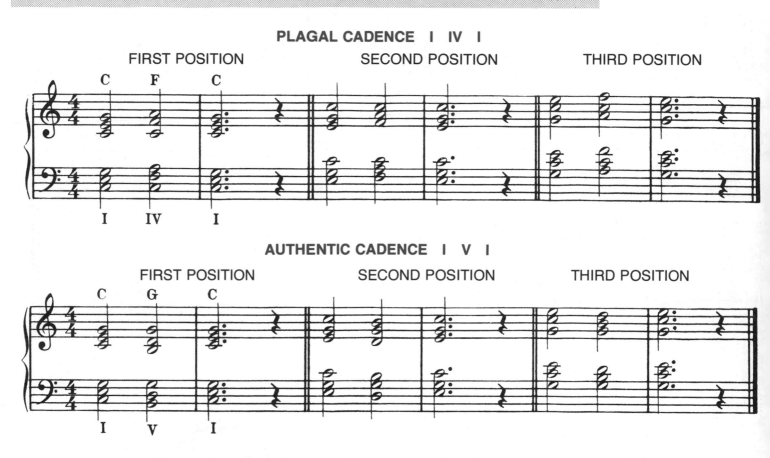

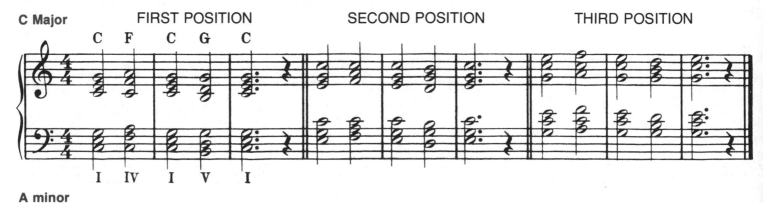

MAJOR SCALES AND PRIMARY CHORDS
(GROUP 3 AND 4 KEYS)

MANUSCRIPT PAPER

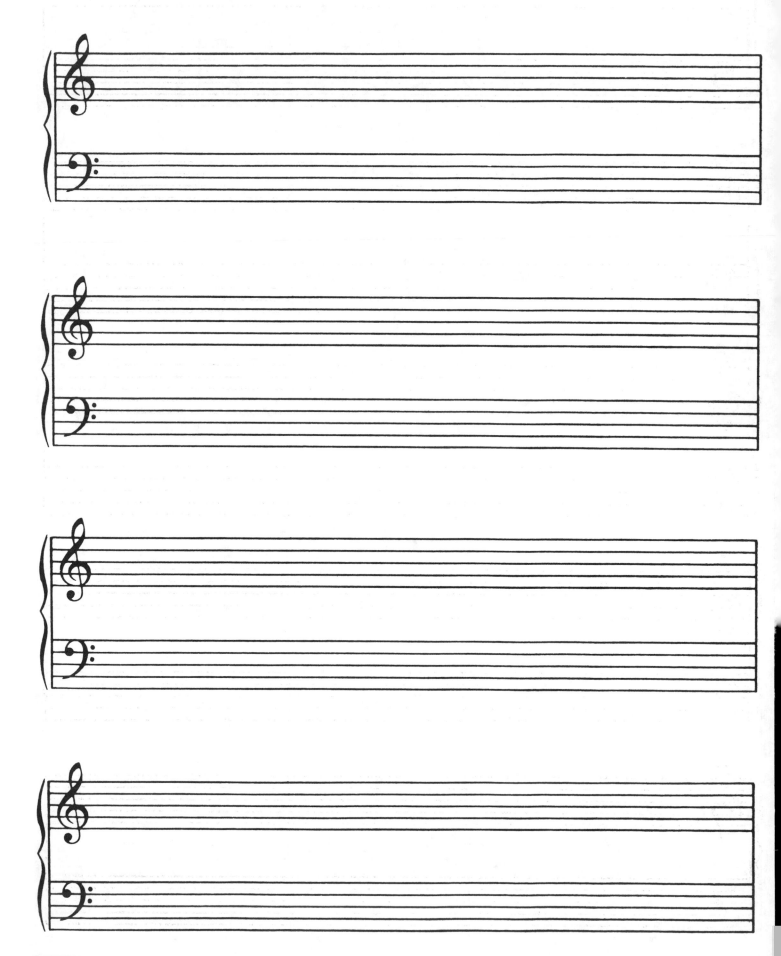